Valerie Vulture's Valentine's Day
Written and Illustrated by Lori Kaiser

Another great book in the Xavier Series!

Published by Carpe Diem Publishers
17401 Betty Blvd.
Canyon, TX 79015
806-433-6321

www.carpediempublishers.com

© Copyright, 2011 by Carpe Diem Publishers. All Rights Reserved. No portion of this book may be reproduced, stored in a retrieval system, or transmitted, in any form or by any means, electronic, mechanical, photocopying, recording, or otherwise without prior written permission from publisher.
Printed in the United States of America
ISBN 978-0-9845761-9-7

To a wonderful friend, Kim...
a terrific writer and a great mom.
Love ya bunches!

Did Valerie Vulture despise valentines?

But all the vultures disliked Valentine's Day.

But getting a valentine was a bit of a dream.

Oh, Valerie wanted a nice valentine;

A big one with candy that read, "please be mine."

For valentine's sake she would make a firm stand.

So Valerie worked, making cards all night long.

It was hard to stay awake being willing and strong.

All the vultures were shocked at what Valerie could make.